The Doctor Will Fix It

by

Bunkong Tuon

The Doctor Will Fix It

Copyright © 2019 by Bunkong Tuon

All rights reserved. No part of this book may be reproduced or transmitted in any form or by any means without written permission of the author.

Library of Congress Control Number: 2019949793

ISBN: 978-0-9600931-4-4

Published by Shabda Press
Pasadena, CA 91107
www.shabdapress.com

For Nicole
the best mom our daughter could ask for

Dear Daughter, Dear Life,
Gender is a construct.
A fiction. Write your own.
Love, Dad

Contents

PART I 1

Thoughts When I Found Out I Was Going to Have a Daughter 3
Life Lesson #23 5
Just Wait and See 6
Moon in Khmer 8
My Daughter Sleeps Tonight 9
Life Lesson # 65 10
Bieber Fever 11
Life Lesson # 77 13
Confession of a Tiger Dad 14
Chanda, the Snow Bomb 15
Two Toys Stand Side by Side 16
Chanda, the Dictator 17
New America 18
Strange Day 19
Chanda's Toy Puppy 20
Dropping Chanda Off at Nursery School 21
Chanda Came Home 22
The ABC's of Race 23
She's Not Like This 24
The Coldness of Other Parents 26
Warm Winter Memories 27
Mantra (or Why I Could Never Be a Good Buddhist) 28
Whatever You Do Don't Let Her Nap Past 4 29
When I Go Out Without My Daughter 31
By the End of the Day Everyone is Cranky 32
The Bite 34
Neighbor 35
Tightrope Dancer 37
Snow Day 38

"Can I Hug You?" 40
A Nightmare 41
Origin 42
Lullaby 43

PART II **45**

The Kind of Father 47
The Other in Me 49
Daddy, Daddy, Fishing? 50
The Walk 52
My Mother on Her Deathbed 53
Important Meeting 55
Women's March in Albany 56
Who is this Child? 57
Identity Crisis of a Biracial Three-Year-Old 58
Look at Me!. 59
No Punk 61
Sunday at the Beach 62
At a Concert 64
Birdsong 65
Ice Cream 67
Glass 69
Coffee 71
Chanda, The Liar 72
Betrayal 74
Swing, Daddy, Swing 76
After a Snowstorm 78
Request 80
Gender Danger 81
Unhappy Father's Day 83
Happy Easter-Cambodian New Year 85
Chanda Says 87
North Star 88
Poetry Doesn't Sell 89

AOL Mail (856)

12/12/2019

Rick
227 Dulude Ave.
Woonsocket, RI 02895

https://mail.aol.com/webmail-std/en-us/suite#

PART I

Thoughts When I Found Out
I Was Going to Have a Daughter

Thank goodness because I have no idea
how to be a man.

Stay away from men—not just the jocks
but even the artsy literary types.
Might as well stay away from women too.
You can live with us, always and forever.

You will be part Greek,
Italian, German, and Cambodian.
More than this, you are our moon and stars
before we even give you that name.

I hope you look Asian like me.
What would people think
if they saw me walking a stroller
with a white baby in it?
That I kidnapped someone's kid?

I hope you don't look Asian
like me.
I don't want anyone, boy or girl,
reducing you to some Oriental fetish.

You will never know
your grandparents on my side.
I hope you will never know the hunger
that comes with such loneliness.

I hope you will never inherit
your old man's troubles.

Forgive me for the mistakes
I will make. There is no user's manual
for anything this beautiful in life.

Life Lesson #23

My wife sits on the futon
laptop on her lap.

Her belly is showing.
The afternoon sun
warms the living room.

I put down my book
and say, "You're beautiful"

"Who are you kidding?"

"The truth compels me
to say these things,"
I say, half jokingly.

But she's not amused.

"You're carrying our child,"
I say. "And I love you"

Just Wait and See

A friend said,
"Strangers will go out
of their way for you."
Another chimed in,
"When I was pregnant
we were at this diner.
The owner came over
with a glass of milk.
I said, 'We didn't order this.'
He smiled, 'For baby.'"
My wife had been waiting
for such moments
but they never came.
Once a young man parked
his black Toyota Tundra
at the entrance of Price Chopper
with the windows down,
Megadeth blasting, cigarette
smoke everywhere.
His girlfriend came out
of the grocery store, leaned
into the window, kissed him,
showing her taut midriff.
My wife walked around them.
At a checkout line the cashier
asked, "How many months
along are you?"
Before she could answer

a young woman behind her
said, "Don't ask her that!"
The two women began
arguing about the etiquette of
assuming a woman
is pregnant.
My wife picked up
her grocery bags
and left quickly,
baby kicking.

Moon in Khmer

You are light
when the sun is punched out
and darkness reigns.
You are the antidote
to what came before:
black blood, black heart,
hands tied, kneeling before
a ditch of human bones.
Your laughter pierces
the silence of night
that bore witness
to the once blood-soaked land.
Your existence is resistance
to the genocide that orphaned
your father and drove
his family out of the homeland.
You are love against
the hate of the Khmer Rouge.
This is the meaning
of your name, Chanda.
This is how to defeat Pol Pot.

My Daughter Sleeps Tonight

My two-month-old daughter sleeps
splayed across the crib with giraffes,
baby elephants, lions, monkeys flying
above her. She's breathing heavily,
snoring. All of a sudden a cry comes
from her upturned lips, right hand turns
to a fist as if she's leading a revolution.

Head with short, dark, spiked hair
shakes from left to right.
Her little body twitches, then stills
for minutes until her clenched fists
flower into soft tiny fingers reaching
beyond the flying animals to catch
stars that only she can see.

My wife and I stand around the crib
fingers clutching its bars.

Life Lesson # 65

My wife and I
are English professors.
But we don't understand
our baby girl.
To communicate
with us, we tell her:
use your words, honey.
Instead, she grunts,
moans, and smiles.
Then farts.

Bieber Fever

My nine-month-old girl
has Bieber fever.
Her head shakes,
puff of hair bounces,
little bum wiggles,
eyes glow, a big smile takes
over as she watches Justin
Bieber on YouTube.
What's a father to do
with lyrics like "I'm missing
more than just your body"?
I click links to Sesame Street,
Big Bird, Cookie Monster,
Elmo, and Ernie
but my daughter loses
interest, crawls to
her pail of toys,
and rummages.

Sixteen years later
the doorbell rings.
A guy who looks like
Kate McKinnon playing
the Bieber on SNL,
jeans torn at the knees,
blond hair spiked,
Siam tiger tattooed on his arm,
smiles his straight white teeth,

shakes my hand, grip firm,
as if he's trying to tell
me something.
My hand dangles
over the front door's sill
until I sense my daughter
beaming from the stairs.
She walks over, kisses
me on the cheek,
then her hand reaches
over to his, holds it.
I watch them walk out,
his manicured hand
around her waist.
She giggles,
pushing him away
playfully.
His black SUV
hums in the night,
in that darkness.

Life Lesson # 77

So much depends
upon
this ten-pound
baby

in her bassinet
arms waving
conducting us,
her dazed orchestra.

Confession of a Tiger Dad

I tell my wife that I want our daughter
to be a doctor.

"You want to be a stereotype?"
She asks.

"Can't an Asian-American father
(note the hyphen) want his daughter

to be a doctor
without risking being a stereotype?"

My wife says nothing.

"You know I'm a curmudgeon when sick!
I just want her to take care of me when I'm old."

Chanda puts her Peppa Pig toy
on the coffee table and turns around.

She stomps her feet, arms on chest,
head shaking, screeching at me,

"No, Daddy. I'm a Mermaid."

Chanda, the Snow Bomb

Chanda undergoes bombogenesis every night.
At three in the morning she screams in her crib
as if she's being chased by a bogeyman.
My wife and I wait to see who will get up
and bring our daughter back to our bed.
Usually it's my wife who cannot bear to hear her cry.
My wife returns cradling Chanda to her chest
whispering, "Baby, Baby, it's all right."
But all night it's not all right for sleep to evade us.
Chanda twists and turns between us
battling a low-pressure system that only her little body
can detect. Every hour she changes location
four to five times, but always perpendicular to us,
forming the letter "H" on our queen-sized bed.
One hour her little toes tickle my nostrils
or heels knead the back of my neck,
and the next her head burrows into my back.
By morning my wife and I wake up sore,
bodies aching, and smiling as we look at Chanda,
hair stuck to sweat-encrusted head, our little queen.

Two Toys Stand Side by Side

A miniature kitchen set
with stove, oven, pots and pans.
A Black and Decker workbench
with screws, hammer, and electric saw.

Sometimes I catch Chanda
at the kitchen in red t-shirt that says
"Keep Calm and Call Wonder Woman"
boiling pink vegetables and plastic sushi.
Other times I catch her standing
at the workbench in her princess dress
sawing a pink Peppa Pig figurine.

Then there are those times
she walks away from the toys,
opens the backdoor, leaves our house,
steps into the sunlight, and laughs.

Chanda, the Dictator

Chanda—towards whom
Everything gravitates
Or the foundation collapses—
Doesn't bark orders
But pleads with her eyes,
Her soft sweet voice,
Hands holding our fingers
'Til we succumb to her demands.
My wife's on all fours,
Meowing like a Kitty Cat.
I'm the lion who roars,
Then licks the dictator's
Palms, tamed.
In bed her knees kneading
My back and shoulders
Until I leave for the guest room
Where I fall asleep
Only to wake up screaming
From a nightmare
Where I lost Chanda
At the beach.

New America

My wife and I are having
breakfast

When our toddler pushes
her potty next to us,

Sits down on her toilet,
grimaces.

When I ask my wife
about her night

Chanda shushes me,
"Quiet, Daddy."

We are stunned at first.
Then we remember how

Our world has changed
since the election.

How civility is shed
and darkness shines.

We turn to our daughter
who now dances like an Apsara.

Unlike that other one,
we adore this little dictator.

Strange Day

Dishes pile high like ancient
minarets in the sink's putrid water.
Chanda wears hummus in her hair
and mustard on her lips. I'm high
from little sleep, hearing bright-colored
aliens speaking a language only my daughter
understands. She's laughing, cracking up.
Those Teletubbies are dancing all morning.
Chanda has on purple boots but there is
no rain outside. In the car seat she plays
with my smartphone, taking photos of her boots
and the back of my head, calling friends
I haven't spoken to in years.
In Hannaford, each time she cries, I reward
her with cookie pieces. She's eaten two whole
cookies and a bag of chips by the time I buy Tylenol.

Chanda's Toy Puppy

Sometimes I call Rosie a "he."
Other times Rosie is a "she."

There's no rhyme or reason
to its gender designation.

All is arbitrary,
dictated by exhaustion.

But what is not fluid
is the proximity of Rosie

to our daughter.

No matter how far away,
we must drive back home

to retrieve the stuffed puppy
I buried under a milk-stained blanket.

Dropping Chanda Off
at Nursery School

Tiny legs wrap around my waist,
tears streaming down her flushed cheeks,
and the wailing "Daddy, Daddy, Home!"
Then the door shuts behind me.
I still hear her crying as I walk by
the classroom window and carry
her crying as I get in the car,
drive to the college to teach
the American/Viet Nam War.
The wailing continues in the cries
of soldiers missing their girlfriends,
wives, and families at home,
wishing to spit at their fathers
who talk about doing the things
men must do in a world of evils,
wanting to burn their town's city hall
and vandalize the draft board
because no one there knows
what they are going through.
The wailing is heard in the little girl
stripped naked by the flaming
fingers of napalm as she runs
with other villagers.
The wailing is felt in the trembling
silence of the boy in My Lai
who hides underneath the warm
bodies of his aunt, younger
sister, and mother.

Chanda Came Home

And told us that a girl from school
had taken away her toys and
hit her. I watched my wife
hold our little girl close to her chest.
The only fight I was ever in:
a sixth-grade girl pushed me
to the ground after I told
the class I had a crush on her.

I spent over a decade
earning advanced degrees,
reading books and gleaning
the wisdom of the ages:
moderation from Ancient Greece,
turning the other cheek from Jesus,
and showing compassion for all life
from the Buddha.

But all I could feel that afternoon
was rage.
I got down on my knees and
to my wife's horror
showed Chanda how to beat the crap
out of another three-year-old girl.

The ABC's of Race

My daughter turns to me
and says, "Daddy, you're brown."

She looks at her mother.
"And you're white, Mommy."

"And what color are you?"
We ask her.

"I'm orange," she tugs
her orange PJ's to show us.

She's Not Like This

My wife says, "She's not like this."
Chanda is kicking the front seat,
as we put her into the car seat,
screaming, "No, No, No School."

Earlier, we took her temperature
after her nose was running and
she said she didn't want to go.
PJ Masks was on the TV.

My wife asks our daughter,
"Does your head hurt?
Does your tummy ache?
Does your back hurt?"

Apparently, she passes our test
by answering the right questions.
My wife turns to me,
"How do we know she's telling
the truth?"

"Like other parenting issues
we have to trust our instincts."
"What do you want to do?"
I pull Chanda out of the car.

I carry my little girl across
the threshold of our home
plant her feet firmly
on the living room floor.

Like a fish off a hook,
Chanda runs to the middle,
turns around, and cries,
"Look at me, Daddy."

She pirouettes on her toes,
dress swirling like a banshee,
arms high, and smiles.

The Coldness of Other Parents

You have seen them in the local park.
There's the father in suit and tie,
hair gelled back, checking his emails,
miles away from his child's laughter.
The yuppie couple sporting windbreakers
and stretchy pants, stare silently at their phones.
Then there's the mother whose daughter stands
near the edge of the playground, no bars to keep
the girl from falling. I move over just in case
the little girl takes a step back and falls.
I watch her go down the slide safely,
feet land firmly on the ground.
The mother notices all this
but says nothing. I want to tell her
that we are in this together,
connected in this crazy world
of parenting, hurled into a hurricane
that rips our flesh, sucks bones
dry and clean like a whistle,
yet we manage to survive,
lifted up by a force not our own.
But the mother, not smiling, pushes
her stroller over to the slide, puts
the little girl in it, heads towards
the swings, leaves Chanda and me
alone in the cold autumn air.

Warm Winter Memories

Much has happened
these last few months.
Two-foot icicles dangling
from rooftop turned our
home into a crystal dungeon.
Then a pipe burst, curled
the kitchen floor, water
seeped into everything.
But this morning Chanda
said "Daddy" for the first time.
I drove home from work.
The sun came out, ice melting.
The Beach Boys on the radio.
I rolled down the car window
& sang "Good Vibrations."

Mantra (or Why I Could Never Be a Good Buddhist)

We are but a drop
in the cosmic ocean.

War is a manifestation
of our greed and lust.

The still point
is the eternal mind

That holds two opposites
and sees them as one.

My still point was
eviscerated the other day.

I mean I *really* lost my shit,
rage took over.

I could murder
someone with bare hands

When Chanda slipped
and scratched her knee.

Whatever You Do
Don't Let Her Nap Past 4

If you do, half of
your night is gone.

But if you don't
life is yours again.

Do as you please.
Read a poetry book.

Watch a film on Netflix
with your wife.

Pick up your neglected guitar.
Learn a pentatonic scale.

Write a novel
or two.

Buy a plane ticket.
Travel the world.

Climb Mt. Everest.
Scuba-dive in Costa Rica.

Watch the sun rise
over Angkor Wat.

Dive off a cliff
in Jamaica.

Base-jump off the tallest
building in Dubai.

Or just sleep,
sweet glorious sleep.

When I Go Out Without My Daughter

The sky is grey. The rain water's cold inside my head.
I don't know who I am anymore.

By the End of the Day
Everyone is Cranky

Chanda is crying for the cartoon show *PJ Masks*
but what she's really crying for is to be in her cozy PJs.
She doesn't know it but she's tired.
Chanda got up at five this morning.
It's a hot summer evening and
who could sleep when it's 90 degrees out?
The garbage melts in the humid air.
Somewhere my students are at some exotic beach
in the French Riviera, in their swimsuits and trunks,
soaking up the sun, jumping into waves,
and splashing water everywhere. And I bow to them,
"Have fun while you're young. You are in
full bloom; the glory of youth is yours."
At the barber today I glanced at the floor
and saw what I didn't want to accept:
the grey was taking over my head.
The sun is finally setting. Chanda still
doesn't want to story time, saying she's thirsty,
she's hungry, she needs to pee,
anything to get out of a night of good sleep,
which is what my wife and I need most right now.
My wife glares at me. Everything
I do annoys her and I'm annoyed that
she is annoyed with me. It's a vicious circle,
a sad dance where our skin is so thin
that our flesh could fall off our bones.
Finally Chanda sleeps. My wife attacks

her dissertation. I go to the shower, undress.
The water splashes against my skin.
My eyes close. I'm smiling like I'm at a beach,
waves lapping my body, washing the grime off,
touching my flesh like I'm being reborn.
These are my hands, five fingers each.
These are my arms, shoulders, and torso.
My head with trimmed grey hair,
my eyes half open, yes, half open!

The Bite

We pay it no attention
until the bite becomes a rash
spreading like a spider web
on the back of Chanda's leg.
Our minds burn like wild fire.
Google becomes our hated
guide as we navigate WebMD,
Mayo Clinic, and CDC.
We study online images,
whisper symptoms like
bad secrets, and compare notes.
We gather contradictions,
argue. Nothing is certain,
only more questions.
We text friends and family.
Is it too late for antibiotics?
What is Lyme disease?
Will this affect our daughter
for the rest of her life?
We wake up the next morning
clutching each other,
sweat drenched our pillows.

Neighbor

We looked out
the kitchen window
staring at the neighbor
with his red snowblower.
"I don't like him,"
I said to my wife.
"Why?" She asked.
"He's like that Eddie guy
from Barfly," I answered.
My wife smirked,
"I don't talk Bukowski."
I tried explaining,
"The dude is always happy
and smiling."
My wife retorted,
"At least he goes out
and introduces himself
to his neighbors."
And I asked,
"But how sincere
do you think he is?"

With our snowblower
refusing to start,
we got out of the garage
shovels in hands.

We bent our backs,
picked up snow,
looked up and saw
our neighbor building
a perfect snowman
with his kids laughing.
My wife grew quiet
watching Chanda play
alone in the snow.

Tightrope Dancer

You climb the five-rung ladder
at the children's playground.

Your mother crouches
below, holding breath.

I stand behind
counting the plastic rungs.

You kick us away,
"I'm a big girl."

Your mother prepares
to catch your fall.

Each day we hold our breath,
cover our mouths with our hands,

close our eyes, and pray.
Of course, we want you to reach

The top, but not too fast.
And not too far from us.

Snow Day

I carry Chanda
across the college campus.

The wind blows sleet
against our faces.

Chanda burrows
her face into my chest.

Snow everywhere.
Years ago,

I was an orphaned
refugee,

raised by my uncles, aunts,
and grandparents.

English tumbled clumsily
off of our Cambodian tongues.

Bullets of whiteness
chilled our brown skins.

How were we to know
about Thanksgiving and Snow Day?

My daughter whimpers,
"I'm cold, Daddy."

Students hurry by. One stops
and asks, "Do you need help?"

I pull Chanda close
to keep us both warm.

"Can I Hug You?"

My wife asks Chanda.

My daughter answers
with a question,

"How much do you love me?"

My wife answers,
"More than anything."

"More than a cow?"

"Sure," my wife says.

"More than a sheep?"
My wife is silent.

Chanda explains,
"Sheep are really soft."

Chanda again asks.
"More than ice cream?"

Again there is silence.

"Ice cream is sweet.
Like you, Mommy."

A Nightmare

Cries pierce through the deepest
black of the night.

My wife on Chanda's bed,
hand soothing our daughter's back.
"What's wrong, baby girl?"

Chanda looks up.
"He didn't give me a kiss."

"Who?"

"Last night, Daddy forgot
to kiss me goodnight."

Origin

Mommy was born in a Greek temple
on the moon, and the moon was in the sun.
And where light bends, a door opens.
Daddy was born in Cambodia when the moon
appeared, shaky with blue water.
Then the sun was in the moon or
the moon was in the sun, mixing it
to make the color Jupiter. That's me.

Lullaby

You must care for these memories.
Hold them close to your heart.
Sing them a lullaby as soft as breath.
Carry them with you wherever you are.

Plant them in the palm of your hands.
Watch them grow and take shape in others,
springing renewals and new beginnings.
This is the hope we share for you.

You are a reminder of what's good
in this world. An antidote to the bitterness
life sometimes brings. Thus we sing
our songs of devotion and praise.

PART II

The Kind of Father

(After Gloeggler's "The Kind of Man")

I am the kind of father who
avoids making eye contact
with other parents
when I drop my daughter off
at nursery school,
the one who crouches
under a classroom window
to make sure she stops crying
before I go to teach.
I am the father who elbows
other parents and scrambles
for a front seat to take
a video of Chanda's pre-
school graduation ceremony.
I am the kind who wants
to beat the crap out of
the nurse sticking a needle
in my daughter's arm.
I am the kind who goes
to Target to buy toddler snacks
and ends up with an inflatable
kiddie pool in the shape
of a white unicorn.
After I tuck her in for the night
I Facebook pictures of us
in that pool, Chanda

holding the pink mane,
me petting giant pink
wings, smiling.
I am the father who tiptoes
into my daughter's bedroom
to check her breathing,
whispers a prayer, then plants
butterfly kisses on her forehead.
I am the kind of father
who gets on hands and knees,
digs dirt with a trowel,
plants flower bulbs,
taps the soil to make sure
they are firmly planted.
Every afternoon
I take Chanda out
to the garden and together
we water the flowers,
me telling her this is how
you take care of life,
how you care for love.

The Other in Me

I have discovered the other in me:
the one that hums when I wake up
at three, holds the handrail, eyes
barely open, walking down the steps
for the milk bottle in the kitchen.
The other in me is greater
than the sum of my wife and me.
The other in me is time itself,
and yet it is not the time
that business people complain
of not having. It's time immemorial,
it's the beginning and the end,
and it's neither of those things.
The other in me doesn't change
shape, shift perspective, argue
for a position, or complain.
The other in me rests beneath
our ribcages, hums, and radiates.
It is true: my daughter has helped
me access the Atman in all of us.

Daddy, Daddy, Fishing?

Like music, these words
lift me from exhaustion,
from those nights when
Chanda wakes up
at three from a nightmare,
hunger, or wet diaper,
from the constant vigilance
for her safety, making sure
she doesn't hit her head
coming down a slide.
Like music, these words
wake me to the here
& now, Chanda
touching my shoulder
as I sit up on the futon.
I fetch the fishing poles
from the shed
and together we drive
to the local pond.
I dig a wriggling worm
out of a plastic cup,
show her how to pierce
it through with the hook
at least three times,
and then I cast.

My arms around her
I explain how to reel
in the line, keep it tight,
and feel whatever pulls
on the other end,
explain how my uncle
was caught and beaten by
Thai police for leaving
the refugee camp to night-fish,
how even in the States
we fish for food, never sport,
when Chanda cranes
her neck, looks left,
hands letting go of the pole,
points to the noise
from a nearby playground,
and says to me,
"Daddy. Look, boys!"

The Walk

Chanda leads the way.
Stick in hand, she takes her steps
with the pure joy that only the innocent
can experience. Driven by curiosity
she pokes at a leaf blackened
from decay, lying lifeless,
forsaken, in our path.
She turns the leaf over.
An earthworm curls sideways,
its slimy body twisted by burning light.
Chanda kneels in front
of the worm and the dead leaf,
and lets go of the stick.
Her hands reach out to touch,
to feel life and
the hurt that comes with it.
I kick the leaf and worm away,
lift my daughter up, and hold her.

My Mother on Her Deathbed

Withered away in pus,
knowing that she'd leave
me, her only child.
My uncle's body crouched in
fetal position on the red
dirt of the refugee camp,
heavy boots of Thai soldiers
thundering on his head,
back and stomach.
Grandmother weeps
at night
for all her children,
alive and dead,
for her orphaned grandson,
for all parents haunted
by helplessness.
In America
I was the new kid,
a reminder of a war
that tore families apart.
Saliva clung
to my tear-stained cheeks
and stuck to my hair.
Stephanie
my first crush said,
"It's nothing personal."
But these memories
are wiped clean.

All is forgiven.
A flower blooms
in the desert
when my daughter
hugs me.

Important Meeting

Instead of the scent of pine
that goes with the hardwood floor,
red ottoman rug, chairs with
leather armrests, portraits of old
white men to remind me of
a certain kind of tradition,
I detected the unmistakable
stench of human waste,
the kind you feel pushing up
your nostrils and seeping into
your brain when you find yourself
in a Porta Potty on a summer
afternoon at a rock concert,
heat bending the sun's rays.
Looking up at me were
deans and department chairs
in suits and ties, power pants
and matching blouses,
my C.V. on the mahogany table.
I took a step back into the hallway
and made way to the restroom
where I scrubbed my brown hands,
sweat dripping from my temple,
sniffing fingers to make sure they
were cleansed of my daughter's poop.
Feeling good, I walked back
into the room but the shitty
smell still persisted.

Women's March in Albany

I take Chanda out of the stroller,
lift her high up over my head,
and put her on my shoulders.

So she can see that she's never alone.
We are here for her, my wife and I,
and other women and men too.

We will march city streets,
climb mountains, and cross rivers
and jungles to let her know.

Our strength is in our love for her.
And her strength is felt in the trembling
ground, the demands for autonomy,

respect and decency, no woman
left behind, in speaking up and out,
in hollering and screaming. In songs.

Who is this Child?

Who sashays across
the grocery aisle?
Who makes a beeline
for the sunglasses rack
and tries on every shade
posing for the store camera?
Who shakes her little bum-bum
when a Katy Perry song
comes on the radio?
Who smiles and talks to strangers
like they are old friends?
When the leg of a chair
is loose,
this child carries her pink box
of pretend tools, gets on her back,
rolls under the chair, and proceeds
to tighten a screw.
Chanda, where did you come from?
Why did you choose for parents
blind mice when it comes to adulting?
It matters none the reasons
we are gifted with you.
You can winterize the lawn mover,
summerize the snow blower,
fix our leaking faucet,
schmooze with college deans
at holiday parties,
and please please please
do our taxes.

Identity Crisis of a Biracial Three-Year-Old

I'm a princess of the world.
No, I'm not a princess of the world.
I'm a human being in the world.
No, I'm not a human being in the world.

I'm Batman; no, I'm Spiderman
I'm Owlet; no, I'm . . .

I'm a mermaid of the sea.
Yes, I'm a mermaid of the sea.

Look at Me!

It'd been raining for several days
the kind that wipes away the dreariness
and disappointments of the summer,
like that time when Chanda becomes
the gender police in our household.
"That pink chair is for Mommy,"
she corrects me.
"You have the blue one Daddy."
Hoping to revise the narrative,
an alternative to the Noah story,
I sit down in the blue chair
and ask my daughter to paint my nails
after she's done with her mother's.
The purple nail polish feels cool
and soothing on my fingertips.

That afternoon I keep admiring
the beauty and elegance of my nails.
When we drive to the grocery store
the nails are bright and screaming,
"Look at me! Look at me!"
I watch my fingers spread
on the steering wheel basking in
the warm sun until my wife yells
from the backseat, "Pretty Hubby!
Keep your eyes on the road!"

The next day I take Chanda
to the local park. Children run,
scream, slide, laugh, climb,
and push. Parents sit on benches,
stand near the slides, chat.
Then I see a group of fathers
standing near the sandlot,
their sons taking turns
handling this toy machine
that digs and scoops up sand.
I clam up. My hands burrow
deep in my pockets, ashamed.

No Punk

The morning coffee
warms up my aching bones.
I pull tight boot strings
brush snow off the old Corolla.
Its engine hums.
I teach morning classes,
wait in my office for no student to show,
and attend a faculty meeting.
Later in the day
I take a third cup of coffee,
grade papers, have a student come by
to argue his grade, and realize
I'm The Man punk bands
give their middle finger to.
I walk back to the parking lot,
clear snow off the car, and drive home
to the magic that is Chanda.
The snow is white
crystal in the sky.
The world is bright good,
a Christmas tree.

Sunday at the Beach

The boy, a child himself,
smile vast as the ocean,
brown hair as wild and
reckless as the waves,
came up to Chanda
who was chasing seagulls,
splashing the salty water,
and stopped her in her tracks.
Chanda turned,
seashells in hand.
He hugged her,
and the shells fell.
His mother smiled
uncomfortably.
I smiled to let her
know it was fine.
Then Chanda looked up
at me,
helplessness in her eyes,
squirming in his arms,
and ran towards me.
I bent down and hugged her.
The boy followed,
waited for Chanda
to turn her head,
then put his palm
on her forehead and pushed
her head back.

The boy walked away
leaving his mother
and me in shock.
Weeks later,
away from waves crashing
and seagulls squawking
my two-year-old girl
said to my wife,
"Hug hurt."

At a Concert

That time you took your three-year-old
to a concert, you didn't realize where
you were until you were deep in it:
Sitting in the middle aisle, on the green lawn,
with the sun dipping behind the place
beyond the pines. The musicians concluded
their performances with "God bless you all"
or "God bless America." The crowd cheered.
Then everything became clear. How you pass
a diner despite your stomach growling
for fear of the unsaid words and the glances
that say so much. The minute you feel American
something always happens to strip that away,
to remind you of your skin, your hair, your flat nose
and you begin to stutter and the accent
tumbles out of your Asian lips like flies.
You looked around in a sea of whites and
your daughter became your life jacket.
She's born in America, her skin whiter.
Your name, your wife couldn't pronounce.
How will your daughter utter it
to claim you as one of her own?
Will you also be foreign
on her American tongue?

Birdsong

Here, in the Northeast,
There is snow on the frozen ground.
Birds are flying from the South,
Crying madly in the mourning sky.
A man with a gun is hunting them.
The branches shake against
Our bedroom window.
Chanda wakes up terrified.
"What's going on, Daddy?"
The birds sing a plaintive song,
Song of sadness and urgency.
My glass window will shatter
If nothing is to be done.
"I'm scared."
Chanda tells me.
The birds sing about a teacher
Crouching in the broom closet
With her high school students.
A survivor says afterward,
"First we thought it was firecrackers.
Then my friends fell down,
One by one."
They sing about the adults
Behaving like children,
Taking no responsibility
To protect the young.
They sing about the children
Acting like adults

Marching to that great mansion,
Lying on cold concrete,
Eyes closed. Some held hands,
Others with hands over their chests,
As if caught dead in prayer.

Ice Cream

I take Chanda
to the local mall,
where she flies
in the bounce house
with other kids,
screaming and laughing.
She climbs up
the slide and rolls
down the cushy steps
She pirouettes
on the piano floor.
Then I take her
to the ice cream place
where we share
a cup of vanilla.
I watch her quietly
shove a spoonful
into her waiting mouth,
tasting the sweetness
on her pink tongue.
Memories of my father
flood, how he lost his wife.
When the Khmer Rouge regime
fell, Grandma was preparing to
take me with her to Thailand.
My father took me out
for ice cream one day.
He was telling me

something important.
That he would follow
Grandma and bring me home.
That he would wait for me.
That he would always . . .
But I couldn't hear a word
he said once the ice cream
exploded in my mouth:
so good, such sweetness.

Glass

The possessed tire
came out of nowhere
as we drove on I-287.
It flew over our Dodge Stratus.
It flew over Chanda's
pack 'n play, crayons and coloring pad,
a stuffed puppy named Rosie.
Our Chanda, strapped in a rear-facing seat,
sucked on a pacifier and stared
at the fast-moving cars and trucks.
It flew over my wife gripping
the steering wheel.
It flew over me
thinking about a paper
for a conference in Akron.
Then I saw the tire,
slow, almost graceful,
slide across the blue sky,
my eyes squinting
from the sun's glare,
watching the tire spin, hit
the grill of a truck behind us,
then ricochet,
spinning with full force
towards us.

Later that night
my wife would ask,
"Would you use your body
to shield our daughter from harm?"
Yes, I told her. But I didn't
tell her how quickly the tire spun in the air
and flew straight at us.
I didn't tell her that I closed my eyes.

Coffee

Cut the vein in this wrist.
And thick black liquid will bubble out.
Matters little if I have five cups
or no coffee at all,
Hands shake just the same,
Body jitters to some invisible music.
Eyes half open, or half closed.
The world is still a blur.
The left turns so far left
that they take on the mantle of the right.
I'm afraid to send out this poem.
Seventeen high school students were killed
on Valentine's Day this year.
I haven't slept in a thousand years,
and I'm only 45.
A year ago, the president signed a bill
making it easier for those suffering
from mental illness to buy guns.
My wife is donating the money
I made from a poetry reading
to a group demanding gun control.
Our baby daughter wakes me up
with her crying.
I hold her to my chest.
My hand is rubbing her back.
Outside, the night is completely black.
No stars in sight.

Chanda, The Liar

The lying comes naturally
nowadays like it's her ABC's.
She does it straight to our faces.
Says her lips are bruised when she wants
a popsicle from the freezer
or that she has a tummy ache
when she doesn't want to sleep.
Just the other day she lied
when we drove past a McDonald's.
Said she needed to go potty.
We made a U-turn, parked, got in.
There was no pee but she made out
with a Happy Meal that included
a plastic polar bear. I said,
"We've been duped by fake poop."
When we got home my wife
and I surfed the net. "Lying
is one of the seven detestable sins,"
said an Internet preacher.
Reading a child psychology website
my wife told me, "Lying is a sign
of intelligence. She now knows
the world is made of self and others.
It's a kind of survival skill."
I thought back to the stories
my grandmother told of an uncle
who was taken away by the Khmer
Rouge because he spoke the truth:

he had studied medicine.
Something that heals was transformed
by truth into something that killed.
The next day Chanda came
running through the door,
her arms stretching to the sky,
and said, "Daddy, Daddy!
Somebody hurt me!"
My wife shook her head
to let me know it was another lie.
But I hugged our daughter anyway,
gave her a big squeeze,
never wanted to let her go.

Betrayal

The boy with the curly hair follows
Chanda around the playground.

He climbs the steps alongside her
and wants to hold hands.

Chanda stops, shakes her head.

But the boy is relentless. He waits on top
of the slide for my daughter to catch up.

Chanda turns around and walks
down the steps. The boy gets up and follows.

The boy's father smiles at me awkwardly.

If I tell Chanda to play nice,
what message am I sending her?

That she is to please the opposite sex
no matter how she feels?

The boy's father finally says, "Not
today, kid. She doesn't want to hold hands."

Then I feel awful.
I was that kid without a date in high school.

And I give in to some imagined fraternity
and nod, "Boy, he's good I should be taking notes."

I don't remember anything afterward.
I put Chanda in the car eat.

My hands tremble. It's too late.
It's the first of many that I will fail her.

Swing, Daddy, Swing

I drive across the rust-red bridge,
pass the tiny post office on my right,
a carved pumpkin from last Halloween
on the front porch, its smile disfigured,
when a giant black pickup cuts in front,
a Confederate flag on its tailgate.
On the bumper are two metallic balls
and a silhouette of a leggy
woman in cowboy boots and hat
blowing the tip of a pistol.
Chanda looks out the window
as we cross into the town park.

At the playground, a family of three—
a father, mother, and a girl
about my daughter's age, curly blonde,
skinny arms and legs—watches us.
The father's belly bursts from
underneath his flannel shirt;
the mother holds her frail
body against the swing set.
Chanda pulls my hand, points,
and cries, "Swing, Daddy, Swing."
We walk over. I put Chanda
on the far side of the swing set,
turn to the family, and smile.
The silence is a razor blade,
cutting through the clouds over

the bridge that divides the city
from this place a few towns over.
We are the faces of a new America:
the father a refugee, Chanda a mixture
of the islands of Greece, the hills of Sicily,
and the green paddies of the Mekong Delta.
But Chanda just screams in delight,
oblivious to history lessons and political tension,
swinging higher and higher with each push,
her laughter maddened by the joy
of being released from gravity,
immune to the rage that consumes me.

After a Snowstorm

The birds are chirping in the morning.
There's been another school shooting.

My wife and I are driving our
three-year-old to her dance class.

Gunfire rings in our rattled minds.
"Temperature is supposed to skyrocket

into the 70s tomorrow.
Strange days we're having,"

I say and take a left on Route 7.
"It's no stranger than anything

else happening in our world,"
Says my wife. I stay on Union.

Pass a McDonalds on our right.
"It's so bright with snow everywhere,"

My wife squints.
Chanda answers from the back seat,

"Mommy, it's not bright. There is no sun.
Oh no! The sun is broken!"

I stop at a red light.
Fingers grip the wheel.

Chanda sighs, "I'm sorry."
My wife and I look at each other.

"But it's OK, Mommy and Daddy.
The doctor will fix it."

Request

The sun glares
through the car window.

Chanda squints.
"Too bright, Daddy."

I shade the window
with a *PJ Masks* towel.

At a four-way intersection
McDonalds is on our right,
and Bruegger's on our left.

"I want paint, Daddy,
to make this city beautiful."

At a bounce house
the boys run amok.

They jump, push, and pull.
Climb the slide the wrong way.

Chanda hides behind me,
squeezes my fingers.

"Make them stop, Daddy."
"Make them go away, Daddy."

Gender Danger

Chanda goes down
the slide, then climbs
back on it, and laughs
when I shake my head,
"No, not that way."
She flies on the zip-line
yells, "Look at me, Daddy."
Inside a giant plastic globe
she screeches as I spin
her world. Then she says,
"Potty, Daddy, Potty."
We cross the lawn,
go through a corridor,
and find ourselves in
front of the bathroom
I move us towards
the men's room
but Chanda yanks me
to the women's room.
She is aware of gender
but is not ready to use
the restroom on her own.
"Daddy can't go in there,"
I explain. She cries, "No
boys' room. No boys."
A woman walks by.
I want to ask for help
but reason prevails.

So I pull Chanda
into the men's room.
She's on the toilet,
tears streaming
down her face.
Someone comes in
right after us, whistling.
Chanda looks at me,
eyes squinting, screeches.
I hold one of her hands,
pat her shuddering
shoulders, and repeat,
"It's okay, Honey.
Daddy's right here."

Unhappy Father's Day

With her mother's hand guiding
Hers, Chanda writes.

I love Daddy Monster.
I like skateboarding with you.

And my favorite,
You are an Owl.

But my joy is mixed with anguish,
Sadness, rage this Father's Day.

Her gift brings up the horrors
Of those parents who are detained,

Who watch their children torn
Away from their trembling hands.

Grown men and women weep.
Some men hang themselves with belts

From Guatemala, Honduras, Nicaragua
Because there is nothing they could do.

I too was just like them:
My uncles, aunts, grandparents took

What they could carry.
Me on my grandmother's back, and we left

Cambodia to seek refuge in America.
How was my family different from theirs?

Legality is but a line drawn across
The desert to keep out the inhuman.

Tents are constructed, and warehouses
Converted into holding cells.

Parents and children are separated,
Placed in corrals like cattle.

A child with a Michael Jordan
T-shirt that says, "Just Do It!"

Convulses as he watches his father
Dragged away by armed officers.

A mother gets down on her knees,
Ties her daughter's shoes

Not knowing if she will ever
Tie them again.

As I hold Chanda my smile
Crumbles. All I hear is

The maddening, blinding roar

Of children crying, women
Weeping, grown men groaning.

Happy Easter-Cambodian New Year

My wife asks:
"What are we going to do
for Chanda this Khmer New Year?"

It's April, and the birds are chirping,
bringing their spring songs to sidewalks
cracked by salt and sun. The cold wind's gone.
I just finished another grueling term
of teaching, meetings, and letter writing.

I scratch my head, and say, "I don't know."

In Cambodia, we'd bring food to the temple, sit to one side
with legs folded, hands clasped in prayer, eyes closed
for a couple hours, then get blessed by Buddhist monks.
There would be music, dancing, and games afterward,
when the young run and laugh and teenagers chase
each other with powder in hands and flirtation in hearts.

But we are in America now.

I tell my wife,
"The closest Cambodian community is in Utica.
I don't have family there."

All that my wife remembers of her church
is sitting through hours-long rituals conducted in Greek,
a language that was cut short when her Yia Yia

decided to speak only English to her children.
That was the American thing to do back then.
That was when America was "great."

We decide to make do with what we have,
the scraps of memory, desire and longing,
the scattering of seeds miles and miles away
from our ancestral lands, the confusion
and tongues cut to be more American.

In the Easter basket of painted eggs
I place a 4 X 6 card with the words
"Happy New Year 2017" in Khmer
alongside another card that reads
"Happy Easter 2017" in Greek.

When Chanda sees the basket
she pulls away the pretty ribbons and
goes for the candies and painted eggs,
leaving the cards written in Khmer and Greek
on the floor, face down.

Chanda Says

"You're the greatest daddy
in the whole wide world."

Her arms wrap tightly
around my neck as she plants

A big fat juicy kiss on my cheek.
For a minute, I almost forgive

The Khmer Rouge. Then I remember
my daughter would never know

Her *Lok-Yiey* and *Lok-Ta*.

North Star

Mariah Carey sings on the radio
for that special someone to be near.
I have my wife, Nicole, and daughter,
Chanda, here in this living room.
My wife stands next to the tree
waiting for Chanda to bring her
ornaments—photos of nephews,
parents and grandparents,
of us on our wedding day,
of Baby Chanda's first Christmas.
Our daughter looks up at the tree:
eyes twinkle, mouth wide and smiling.
When I was a kid, Christmas happened
to other families, mostly white,
mostly Catholic, evening mass,
solemn prayer at the dinner table.
Christmas was what I saw
on the television: Bing Crosby
dreaming of a white Christmas,
Nat King Cole roasting chestnuts
on an open fire, and that crazy
George Bailey-Jimmy Stewart
running on snow-covered streets
wishing everyone Merry Christmas.
Mariah's voice soars on the radio.
My wife puts a bow in Chanda's hair.
Our daughter sits in her red dress
fingers caressing her mom's elbow.
I put an ornament on the tree.
Night bursts with a thousand quiet stars.

Poetry Doesn't Sell

It doesn't put food on the table.
It doesn't pay for your auto and life insurance,
your medical bills and mortgage expenses.
It doesn't send your children to college
or set up your retirement fund.
It doesn't help a friend dying
of cancer.
It doesn't fix a leaking roof,
help buy a brand new car.
It doesn't even mean
what it says half the time.
Poetry is your daughter looking up,
saying "Daddy" for the first time.
It is after apple picking one afternoon
in a tiny studio near the university
you and your girlfriend were making
sandwiches and you touched her hand.
She turned around, rested her head
on your chest. You breathed in
her autumn hair. She smelled so sweet,
tender, and warm. It wasn't the Macy's
perfume you bought her last Christmas.
It was her. Right then, you knew
she would be the mother of your daughter.

Acknowledgements

I'm grateful to Carol and Jim McCord for their friendship, generosity, and support over the years. My thanks to the English Department at Union College, with our fearless leader Bernhard Kuhn at the helm; to my colleagues and friends who took time out of their summer to read versions of this manuscript, especially Kara Doyle, Pattie Wareh, and Judy Lewin. I'm also grateful to Union College for a course release to work on this book, particularly for the support of Dean Jenny Fredricks. My many thanks to the folks in my poetry group: Jim McCord (again), David Kaczynski, Malcolm Willison, and Luis Martinez. A special thanks to Teresa Mei Chuc for her unwavering support and enthusiasm for this project. For their friendship, I am thankful to the Misfit poets: Tony Gloeggler, Alan Catlin, Clint Margrave, Ted Jonathan, Alexis Rhone Fancher.

As It Ought to Be Magazine: "Ice Cream," "Gender Bender," "The Bite," "Tightrope Dancer," "Women's March in Albany," "My Mother on her Deathbed"
carte blanche, "Moon in Khmer"
Cultural Weekly: "Just Wait and See"
Chiron Review: "Poetry Doesn't Sell" and "Swing, Daddy, Swing"
Coffee Poems: Reflections on Life with Coffee: "Coffee"
Glass Poets Resist: "Unhappy Father's Day"
Journal of Southeast Asian American Education and Advancement: "Chanda Says" and Dropping Chanda Off At Nursery School"
Luna Luna: "Confession of a Tiger Dad"
Misfit Magazine: "Happy Easter-Cambodian New Year"
New Verse News and *Albany Poets*: "Birdsong"
Paterson Literary Review: "The Kind of Father" and "Glass"
Poetry Quarterly: "My Daughter Sleeps Tonight"

Rattle Poets Respond: "My Daughter, the Snow Bomb"
Shrew Literary Zine: "Two Toys Stand Side by Side"
Small Orange: "Identity Crisis of a Biracial Three-Year-Old"
Nasiona Review: "Thoughts I Found Out I Was Going to Have a Daughter,"
"Sunday at the Beach," and "Chanda Came Home" won the 2019 Nasiona
Nonfiction Poetry Prize
Yellow Chair Review: "Life Lesson # 88"
Yes Poetry: "My Daughter's Toy Puppy"

CPSIA information can be obtained
at www.ICGtesting.com
Printed in the USA
LVHW091124081219
639812LV00002B/467/P